D0771166

Illuminations

Illuminations

Living by Candlelight

Wally Arnold

Produced by Bonnie Trust Dahan
Photographs by Sean Sullivan
Text by Stefanie Marlis
Styling by Anthony Albertus
Design by Sandra McHenry Design

CHRONICLE BOOKS
SAN FRANCISCO

Library of Congress
Cataloging-in-Publication Data available.

ISBN 0-8118-3072-1

Printed in Hong Kong.

Produced by Bonnie Trust Dahan
Text by Stefanie Marlis
Photographs by Sean Sullivan
Styling by Anthony Albertus
Designed by Sandra McHenry Design

Distributed in Canada
by Raincoast Books
9050 Shaughnessy Street
Vancouver, British Columbia
V6P 6E5

10 9 8 7 6 5 4 3 2 1

Chronicle Books LLC
85 Second Street
San Francisco,
California 94105

www.chroniclebooks.com

Many thanks to all the kind and hospitable people who welcomed us into their homes:

Kathy and Wally Arnold
Jacquelyn Baas and Stephen Walrod
Deborah Bishop and Michael Liberman
Nan and Bill Cox
Karin Dilou
Jim Dorsey
Jeff Gibson and Neil Ward
Helie Robertson
Gerald Reis
David Salinitro
Phil Schlein
Gloria and Sean Sullivan
Paulette Sun and Michael Davis
Lloyd Tupper
Sloat Van Winkle

A special thank you for their support and help goes to Gerald Reis, Sarah McFadden, Kurt Gilbertson, Yael Dahan, and at Pierre LaFond in Santa Barbara, Celia Denig and Shelley Koury.

Acknowledgments

There are people who must be thanked because without their undertaking, this book would have simply remained an untold story. There are also people without whom there never would have been a story to tell in the first place. Here, I will endeavor to thank them.

Our producer, Bonnie Dahan, belongs in both categories. As the producer of this book she was a visionary and taskmaster wearing both hats with confidence and style. Bonnie, as my colleague at Illuminations, was also the creative force behind many of the products and ideas on these pages. She is a valued friend and taste police. I'm sure the Illuminations library of books will now flourish under her direction.

When I first met our writer, Stefanie Marlis, *Illuminations* was just an idea. Upon hearing the description of what we were to be, Stephanie wrote the words "living by candlelight" that serves to this day as the organizing principle for what we do. She is a talented poet, a generous listener, and wordsmith extraordinaire.

Photographer Sean Sullivan's work speaks for itself. He captures the feeling behind the image with a rare combination of artistry and whimsy. Thank you again for memorializing our essence on film.

Stylist Anthony Albertus has the unique talent to add or take away just what is necessary to make the difference between a photo and an experience. Thank you again for your impeccable style.

Designer Sandy McHenry brought a refreshing Zen-like style of design and communication to this project. Never rushed, always calm, she has presented the work of the above artists with elegance and grace.

To my 1,700 colleagues who work with me at Illuminations and particularly to Michael and Paulette Sun Davis, thank you for dreaming this dream with me.

To every customer we have served, thank you for allowing us to play.

To my wife Kathy and children, Michael, Ted, Nick, Chris, and Sam, thank you for sharing me and supporting me.

Finally, I wish to especially thank Minnie Perkins for teaching me at an early age that I could be anything I wanted.

Contents

Both the dining room and living room are lit with candles in this adobe house. After dinner, guests can lean back and relax as pillar candles in Moroccan lanterns and votive candles in Moroccan tea glasses bring the warmth of candlelight to the New Mexican–style hearth.

Introduction

"Let the beauty we love be what we do." ~ R U M I

My relationship with candlelight was never about candles. Instead it was all about illumination. ❧ The story began one day in London, England. I was an entrepreneur on a mission. I had decided to create a new business and had set aside one day in my busy life to walk through the streets of this remarkable city and make a discovery. ❧ I awoke in my hotel room, ordered some breakfast and got ready for the day. At one moment, doubt crept in and I thought to myself how ridiculous it was to think I would really discover something that day. Nevertheless, I decided to carry on with my plan, choosing instead to fully consider all possibilities. ❧ Wandering in and out of dozens of shops, I did not know what I was looking for, simply trusting my intuition as my guide. The seminal moment came in the mid-afternoon as I ventured down Oxford Street and chose to enter a small, nondescript store. Drawn in by the scent, I encountered a lit candelabra that cast its glow about the room. ❧ As I looked at that living light, dancing in front of me, transforming the space around me, I knew in my heart that the discovery had been made. In that moment, without knowing it, I became a steward both for candlelight and what would later become a company called Illuminations. ❧ Prior to my epiphany, I was not a candle connoisseur; my candle experiences were limited to the holiday season and birthday cakes. Not one to hold myself back, I dove headfirst into this new world. ❧ I wondered who *really* lived by candlelight in this modern era when it is a choice and not a necessity. I discovered that in Europe candlelight continues to be part of daily life in millions of homes throughout many countries. ❧ In these homes, where candlelight lives, one might also find fresh flowers from the garden, meals prepared with ingredients bought at the market that same day and a quality and pace of life that is often missing in America. ❦ In America, I observed, perhaps our greatest freedom is that anyone can be anything, limited simply by desire and drive. However, as we go about the creation of who we will be, one price we sometimes pay is that we forget to live. ❦ In a culture that richly rewards achievement and accomplishment, it is left to us to create a balanced life, to master the art of creating a life worth living. ❦ I could easily use these pages to share the many stories about the creation of Illuminations. How doubters were prevalent and believers were scarce. How we thought we knew something and discovered we knew less than we thought. How challenging and yet rewarding it is to remain true to one's intention. To dwell on those things would be to miss the point, the true illumination. ❦ Simply said, candlelight is a tool that we are connected to at our deepest levels. Part of our ancient memories, it can transform our homes and our lives when we use it to create balance in our day. ❦ You can transform your meals, your bath, your bedroom, your garden, and your relationships when you bathe and nurture them in candlelight. A perfect gift for yourself and your loved ones, candlelight, like music, is a universal language. It is understood by all and communicates without words. ❦ As you go about your process of creating a life worth living, it helps to remember it is a simple daily practice, because you live only one day. It is that single day, well lived, where you create a balanced and fulfilling life. ❦ In your pursuit, consider this lesson shared by a friend who once met a master Zen archer and observed him shooting arrow upon arrow, perfectly in the center of his target. My friend asked the archer, "How long did it take you to develop such skill?" ❦ The archer replied, "You mean, how long did it take me to realize there is only practice." ❦ Therein lies the essence of illumination. ❦

~ *Wally Arnold*

Once you start living by candlelight, you begin to see more and more places where candlelight could lend its transformative magic. Certainly the style of your home will influence the style of the candles and candle accessories you bring to it, but any home, whether a country house or city house, whether contemporary or traditional, will start to inspire you. Soon you'll find that even something as simple as a pair of dinner candles set on a windowsill, can, in a small way, change your world.

At the Table

The Old Masters appreciated the beauty of candlelight at the table, and in painting after painting, we see glowing, candlelit faces looking up from a meal. For centuries, of course, candles, or oil lamps, were a necessity. In winter, they were often lit for both breakfast and dinner. But today, since they're an option, they are a more apparent pleasure—and the possibilities for using candles inventively are endless.

The kind of candles and candleholders that you bring to the table are as much about style as the food you bring. Ivory pillars shining through glass cylinders dressed up with shimmery fabric sleeves might well suit a meal where Indian or Moroccan food is being served, transporting guests to a table on the other side of the world. A traditional Japanese meal might be brought to a bare wooden table-top where lotus-shaped floating candles have been set adrift in a dark-bottomed bowl. Begin the evening with a reading of a haiku about the moon, and suddenly it's ninth-century Japan, and guests are enjoying a quiet meal before going out to moon-gaze. ❧ Candles are appropriate at any table, and they're de rigueur for formal dinners. Tall tapers take their place right alongside full table settings and fine wines. Place a pair of ivory ones in a pair of silver candleholders on a white linen tablecloth, and you instantly make an elegant statement. With candles on the table, dining alfresco can be equally gracious. Use votive cups as place markers at a garden party. Turn Tuesday's macaroni-and-cheese supper into a memorable family event by lighting the kitchen table with unscented pillar candles. Take advantage of the first warmer, longer evenings of the year with a candlelight picnic on the lawn. Or, take your picnic to the beach by planting a half-dozen votive stakes in the sand around a spread tablecloth. Wake up early and watch the sun rise while having a candlelit breakfast in bed or on your balcony. In the fall, place a wide-mouthed bowl filled with water and leaf-shaped floating candles in the center of a table—artful, even when unlit, at any time of day. For the most part, it's best to burn unscented candles at the table, but that doesn't mean uncolored ones—candles without fragrance come in dozens of colors and shapes. After dinner—or after cooking—you may want to burn scented candles; there are even candles that have no discernable scent of their own but clear the air of such unpleasant ones as smoke or fish. ❧ At supper in the kitchen or a romantic dinner for two on a city rooftop, candles work their magic, casting an inimitable light over all. Conversations deepen, and the food on the table before us looks even more delicious. At any time of day, candles at the table are the visual equivalent of saying grace. They honor the beauty of being alive and the bounty we share. ❧

Though we have a tendency to associate candles at the table with dinner by candlelight, lighting candles for a daytime affair, such as this afternoon buffet, is equally enchanting. A white and ivory palette sets a more formal mood. Iridescent candle sleeves slipped over glass cylinders and votive cups give the event extra shimmer.

What to Look for in a Candle

All candles are not created equal, nor do they burn equally. The quality of a candle depends on how it's made and what it's made of. Look for candles made with wax, wicks, and fragrances that are contaminant-free. Candles made with purified paraffin wax—what is known as food-grade—are the best choice. The wick is as important as the wax. Though American candle manufacturers have not used lead wicks for nearly twenty years, European and Asian companies still do, and some of these candles find their way here. Fortunately, there's a way to find out if a candle's metal wick contains lead. Simply rub the wick against a piece of paper; if it leaves a pencil-like mark, you know it contains lead. Since not all metal wicks do contain lead, it's worth checking. Some paper wicks need to be supported with zinc stems; zinc, however, is lead-free.

There are other considerations besides ingredients. For instance, some colored taper candles are a solid color throughout, while others have a white core with color on the outside. The latter method makes a stronger candle, as solid-color candles absorb sunlight and heat more readily and, therefore, are more likely to bend. When purchasing aromatherapy or filled candles, make sure that their fragrances are derived naturally, from flowers and plants. Also, when shopping for a filled candle, you'll want to bear in mind that the optimum height is about four inches—any taller and the candle is apt to smoke. No matter how good the quality of the fragrance or wax, the candle simply won't receive the oxygen it needs. As with all candles, the quality of a filled candle is put to the test when you burn it.

Lighting designers are very conscious of just where the light from one fixture ends and another's begins. In designing your own candlelit settings, illuminate not just the table and the food you bring to it, but your guests' faces as well by placing candles at various elevations.

Candlelight inspires invention. Here, tea lights are paired with cut-glass wineglasses. The interplay of candles, with their trembling flames, and reflective glass bespeaks a novel elegance, yet it couldn't be easier to achieve.

An unscented floating candle rests on the still water inside a small glass cylinder made all the more scintillating by an iridescent mesh sleeve. Light one at every place setting, or set these beautiful little worlds randomly all around the table.

Colorful glass votive cups are the focal point of this unusual chandelier. A cheerful alternative to electric lights, the votive candles will burn all afternoon and late into the evening, shining jubilantly above any table. If you can't find the candle accessory you have in mind, consider taking an electric fixture and adapting it for candlelight.

At the center of a rustic kitchen table, spring's first poppies sprout from a ceramic vase, its glazed surface gleaming with reflected light from the votive candle by its side. Candles have a way with flowers. Even pastel petals take on a vibrancy and seem to have a second life in candlelight, after the first in sunlight.

Breaking the rules with candles can be especially rewarding. Mixing different types of candles—here votive candles and dinner candles—and accessories can create a quirky effect that feels just right. The mix of dinner candles and holders, individual votive candles, and a handcrafted chandelier in this country kitchen supply all the light and the perfect ambience for a casual but unforgettable family supper.

Give some forethought to the location of your alfresco meal. Scout out the possibilities, bearing in mind elements such as sun, shade, wind, and the sounds of the neighborhood. A quiet, semi-sheltered place like this doorway is ideal for a table for two or a small gathering.

There's no end to the variety of inland seas on which to set sail floating candles. For instance, this brass *urli*—a large Indian cooking pot—has been filled with water and a platoon of light-hearted tea lights in floating holders. Part of the beauty here is the juxtaposition of the delicate, dancing lamps with the somber metal of the pot.

An alfresco meal can be wholly impromptu: If the sun comes out, move lunch outside. Keep both the food and the table setting simple, and the candlelight expressive. A favorite wine completes the scene. With votive candles in glass holders and a large hurricane lamp on the table, and a hanging lamp above, neither stray breezes nor diminishing light will interfere with this open-air dinner.

Ivory pillar candles in hurricane lamps and votives in glass cups will lend a warm glow to the faces of host and guests, while the light from the *hundai* chandelier will make plates of food look all the more appetizing. Whenever you're pairing food and candles, it's best to use unscented candles so as not to overpower the smells and tastes of the food you're serving.

Just as it would indoors, this glass and metal chandelier provides excellent overhead outdoor lighting. *Hundai* chandeliers, like this one, were brought to India from Belgium in the early 1900s. Before being converted to electric fixtures, they were used as oil lamps. This one holds a single pillar candle.

The massive stone wall is a key element of this country home's architecture. More votive candles in glass holders define the boundaries of this makeshift dining room and punctuate the rocky face of the wall. Each holder sits securely on a piece of wood that has been wedged into one of its many crevices.

This graceful vine of small glass teardrop lamps frames the bold stone doorway, setting the stage for a romantic meal. The lamps protect the votive candles from breezes, so fixtures like this are perfect to use outdoors. Let the candles inside burn down; the next day, remove them and replace them with flowers.

It takes some thought, but it's possible to light a room entirely by candlelight. In this room, ten three-inch pillar candles of varying heights set on the prickets of a hand-wrought iron chandelier provide all the overhead lighting. More pillar candles in twin glass hurricane lamps and dinner candles in a pair of rusted urns, salvaged from the garden, offer tabletop illumination.

Three two-inch pillar candles in footed ironwork pillar holders, on the sideboard of this same wine-country dining room, show an oil painting in a most flattering light.

A hurricane lamp has both a practical and a romantic side. It keeps a candle's flame from being extinguished and from burning unevenly in unexpected drafts, and it does so in a most gracious way. At this table, two large fluted glass hurricane lamps act as elegant anchors.

We do more at tables, of course, than enjoy meals together. At this one, on a rooftop with a panoramic view of city and bay, the stage has been set for gift giving. The table is actually outside an office; candlelight at the workplace is a thing of beauty that can remind us, in the midst of harried days, to take a deep breath.

A linen tablecloth, a bouquet of ranunculas and lilacs, placed next to small and large lanterns with metal lattice and translucent Capiz shell panes, each holding a votive cup, all conspire to make the occasion a memorable one. Beautifully translucent Capiz shells, which are found in abundance in the deep waters of the Philippines, were used for centuries as windows in more elegant homes.

For those who prefer to sit somewhere other than the ground, set a few small lanterns on and around a bench. Mix in flowers, such as pansies, in colorful pots. The rectangular lanterns on this bench have tinted glass faces and zinc frames. Zinc works well outdoors; as architects and florists know, it's a resilient metal that weathers beautifully.

As the lanterns used at this picnic demonstrate, there are an infinite number of ways to protect candles from the wind. These fanciful lanterns, with their globes of colored glass, gleam with a votive candle that will provide up to ten hours of light. Though the twilit Shangri-la pictured here took some creative thinking, it was fun thinking.

Arranging a candlelight picnic may call for a bit of reckless abandon. If you like the whimsy you see here, don't worry about what goes with what. The whole idea is to have fun. Throw a blanket out on a deck or on a lawn under a tree, and start hanging every kind and every shape of lantern imaginable. You might even throw in a few Chinese paper lanterns like the ones you see here, though you wouldn't want to put candles in them.

Let your artistic inclinations rule. Your house is bound to have a nook or unadorned corner where you can create a vignette like this autumnal one. Squash and pumpkins—treasures of the autumn harvest—are lit with votive candles in clear glass holders and made all the more interesting by a small framed print. If you're familiar with the work of Joseph Cornell, you might well note a similarity.

Butternut squash, white pumpkins, turban squash, gourds: These sisters and brothers of the more usual organic candleholder, the pumpkin, with their intriguing shapes, colors, and textures, invite sculpture at the table. Mix your media by adding the magic of candlelight.

It's Thanksgiving, and you're going to be cooking all day long. Why not brighten the ambience of the kitchen and provide yourself with some inspiration? Begin with a small, perhaps imperfect, table. Add a pretty tablecloth. Now you've got a wonderful backdrop for an original candle garden to remind yourself, and anyone who comes into the kitchen, of the bounty that inspires the day.

29

Translucent as they are, floating gel candles inside a wide hand-blown bowl cast a shimmer like sunlight on the surface of a lake. These gel candles are long-burning, which makes them exceptionally economical. The clear lamps and glass bowl reflect the colors of the flowers and the flames of other candles. An elegant Sunday brunch demands candlelight.

Take advantage of a side table by using it as a blank canvas. This window table with its highly reflective surface has been lined with antique books and expressive offerings from the spring garden. Orchids contribute a composed grace. Candlelight adds the finishing touch that turns the dining room into a work of art.

Don't underestimate the potential of tea lights. Used generously, they are a pennywise way to provide plenty of table-level light. They contribute, too, a whispered liveliness. Arranged in a fluid pattern in the simplest transparent holders, it's as if the tea lights used in this dining room were dancing around the bouquets of fresh-picked flowers.

Candlelight weaves its soft magic in this urban loft space, taking the edges off what might otherwise be an overly austere environment. Hand-wrought in black metal, the candelabra at the center of the table displays a spectrum of handmade pillar candles.

Several of these metal and glass votive cups contribute more character to the table setting. Colored glass votives march up the stairs, bringing the spirit of the evening to the rest of the living space. Suspended above the table is an electrified chandelier that coordinates beautifully with the candle accessories.

A little closer to the center of the table, chromatic dinner candles held by bronze candlesticks flank a scrollwork candelabra and lend a steady gleam to the festive glasses and petal plates. This playful kaleidoscope is mirrored in the long stainless-steel tabletop.

Gathering Light

People have been gathering around fires and candles for eons. But even for our Paleolithic forebears, fire-light, and later candlelight, was more than a physical necessity. The communal fire, family hearth, or candlelit dwelling provided a social center. It gave people a place to be together: to share hopes and dreams, to tell tales, and to confess their innermost feelings.

In contemporary houses, the family room, living room, and den have taken the place of central rooms with traditional hearths. That's one reason that they lend themselves so well to candlelight. Just as the cave dweller's fire drew others toward it, so does a quartet of pillar candles burning on stone plates on the family room coffee table. A den lit with candlelight can be wonderfully cozy; small candles placed in nooks and crannies all around the room draw us into a family circle or circle of friends. ❦ When it's time to have heart-to-heart encounters, candles can be of real service. They can be used instead of a "talking stick" to remind people to really listen to one another. Only when it's your turn to light a candle placed in front of you is it your turn to speak. ❦ Sometimes, it takes a stormy night and a power outage to rekindle our appreciation of living by candlelight. A living room is marvelously transformed by two dozen votive candles set about the room. The family comes together; fears are dispelled as stories are woven. ❦ There's certainly no reason to wait for catastrophe, however. Candlelight has a magnetic effect. Light a candle anywhere in the house and watch how people gravitate there. ❦ If lighting the whole living room with candlelight seems too ambitious, just light a conversation area where friends can share a glass of wine that glows with the subtle warmth candlelight imparts to it. Somehow, candlelight manages to change our perception of time. Our attention shifts away from the "world of doing" to the "world of being," and good friends or families sharing an evening by candlelight are apt to find that deeper thoughts float to the surface and that conversations wander late into the night. A conversation lit by candlelight seems to feel more real, more alive. ❦ Music and candlelight are another mood-setting pair. Put on your favorite CD and get lost in the steady flame of a single candle or the shimmer of floating candles adrift in a porcelain bowl. ❦ As any reader knows, books are portals to faraway places and bridges to lofty thoughts, and candlelight can help to light the way. A library bright with candles takes on a transcendental glow. Pull a book down from the shelf and read a story aloud. Have a poetry reading by candlelight. Music, or the music of beautiful language illuminated by candlelight—what a treasure to share. ❦

Think about candles and candlelight when you're remodeling your home or designing a new one. If you love candles, you'll want to build in special places for burning them, such as the stucco window seat next to the fireplace you see here. Knowing that you'll want to bring candlelight into a room can guide your choices from the start.

These lanterns are ubiquitous in Morocco, too. They line the streets of the busy Casbah marketplaces, the *shuk*, which is where you can purchase the tea glasses as well.

In Morocco, everyone drinks tea, all day long. You'll find people sipping tea from glasses like these; most likely they're enjoying a sweet elixir of gunpowder green tea, sugar, and fresh mint. Though unscented votive candles are burning in these, a few drops of mint essential oil could be added to evoke the "taste" of Moroccan life.

An artful arrangement of black wire baskets complements the hammered metal trunk, which takes the place of a more traditional coffee table. The baskets have solid bottoms that act as candle plates and are filled with colored pillar candles chosen to coordinate with the overall decor.

Like the tall redwood trees
that surround the house, almost everything here is oversized—from the wicker
rockers to the tall white calla lilies and
potted fern. And then there are the
votive candles. Placed in traditional glass
votive cups set inside drinking glasses,
they enliven both side table and railing.

Even though the lanterns on
the square columns of this colonial-style
verandah are electric, this sitting area is
especially cozy. Tall triple-wick and
single-wick pillar candles burn in large
glass cylinders filled with colorful green
split peas and white beans.

Glass cylinders act as exceptional windbreakers for candles, and these large ones make it possible to enjoy even the biggest multiwick pillar candles outdoors. They're not a substitute for your attention, however; do keep an eye on candles wherever and whenever you burn them.

You don't have to depend on a specialty store to find the perfect candle holder. Shop creatively and keep in mind that everything from an antique bottle to an art deco drinking glass to a silver vase can make a striking candleholder. Some of the pillar holders in this candlelit living room are vintage silver-plated vases and serving trays that have been given a new life.

Though your local antique store may not think of old lighting fixtures as anything but that, you can be more imaginative. Generally, adapting older electric fixtures for candles is simply a matter of cutting or pulling out the electrical cords. Fixtures with tinted glass, such as this one, lend muted light an Old World feeling.

Though of a decidedly different ilk than most of the decor and candle accessories in this living room, this green ceramic pot/candleholder has its own distinct charm. It's a one-of-a-kind piece designed to hold a ring of dinner candles (here you see beeswax candles dyed with natural color). You, too, could commission a ceramic artist to create a special candle-holder as original as this oddly endearing pot.

Tall tapers in elongated copper candlesticks echo the flames of the roaring fire and lead the eyes upward to their very tips. Right, a selection of pillar candles, including a triple-wick one, are equally captivating. Remember to burn pillar candles long enough to let the pool of melted wax reach the sides of the candle.

The element of shape is not lost on the makers of fine candles. These teardrop candles are a style popular in Paris, the City of Light, a century ago. Seated in equally sculptural candlesticks, they appear even more exotic, helping to set the tone of the evening.

It's been a long day, and tomorrow promises to be equally full; having people over for dinner is out of the question, but sharing an after-dinner wine and plate of fruit is just what's needed to add a dash of pure pleasure to the evening. Elegant candles and a favorite dessert wine can turn a sitting room into a Parisian bistro.

Windows and water amplify the shimmering effects of candlelight as they mirror both candles and flames. This glass dish on a bronze metal base is filled with water and several floating candles. It's thoughtfully placed to reflect both the light from the branchlike metal chandelier and the teardrop candles behind it.

On a warm summer night, enjoy your garden—
no matter how small it is—by candlelight. Candlelight brings
conversations to life. It makes us more attentive not only to
the beauty around us, but also to one another. In this vest-
pocket city garden, large galvanized metal lanterns are hung
with hooks from trees and latticework, and perched on a table
surrounded by votive cups. Part of the charm of candlelight in
the garden is the iridescent quality it gives greenery and
flowers. It's as if we were suddenly privy to their secret life.

A hexagonal stone urn filled with sand or potting soil and topped with colorful stones becomes even more interesting with the addition of votive candles in glass votive holders. The candlelit stones take on a polished look; sea glass is an apt alternative.

These lanterns faced with wire mesh instead of glass have a clear advantage for summertime use. They protect the votive cup, but unlike glass, the ventilating mesh won't heat up—which makes a refreshing difference on balmy summer evenings.

Citronella-scented candles are a practical choice for outdoor use. A tropical Asian grass, citronella has pungent lemon-scented leaves that yield an oil used as a natural insect repellent. Candles imbued with citronella oil have a refreshing, citrusy scent and will dissuade unwanted insects from joining your garden gatherings.

Small galvanized buckets and glass holders arranged on a rough-hewn table illuminate an unstudied still life. A small classical stone urn filled with oranges proffers a counterpoint in color and shape.

A half-dozen votive candles in glass votive cups surround a copious bouquet of tulips. The tulips accentuate the mauve-colored tiles of this unique Moroccan-style table. Like a six-pointed star, the candlelight illuminates both.

The oversized molded-glass square vases on the coffee table sparkle with the light from pomegranate pillar candles. The center cylinder contains a triple-wick one; tea lights burn inside the twin cubes.

More votive candles in glass votive cups outline this contemporary couch and help to define the room's conversation area. One of the bonuses of using candlelight is the unexpected element of design; here, the votive candles cast their reflection on dark, smooth leather.

Beeswax Candles

Unbleached beeswax is long-burning, has a high melting point, and is naturally aromatic, emanating a light fragrance akin to honey. Because the molecular structure of beeswax is denser than that of paraffin, beeswax candles require thicker wicks, which must be trimmed carefully and consistently to ¼ inch in order to prevent smoking. Beeswax is limited in supply and quite expensive; it can also contain unknown impurities picked up from sprayed crops as the bees pollinate them. It's hard to determine the source of the beeswax in a candle, and finding an organic source for beeswax may well be impossible. Much of it is imported, which makes it even more difficult to determine the conditions under which it was gathered and processed.

It's easy to understand why beeswax candles are costly. It takes 500,000 bees traveling 150,000 miles to produce the fifty pounds of honey whose combs become one pound of beeswax. Beeswax is best suited for solid tapers, dinner candles, and pillars. The purest beeswax candles come in natural colors: light honey to dark amber to pale shades of green. All pure white and slightly off-white beeswax has been bleached. A hundred years ago, it was bleached naturally in troughs placed in the sun, but today, the bleach is simply poured into the tanks of wax. You can find pure beeswax candles of good quality if you stay away from the bleached variety and, as with any candles, purchase them from a reliable purveyor.

Beeswax candles are long-burning and scent the air with a delicate honeyed fragrance. Many of the candles you see here are made with beeswax. You'll notice classic tapers, twisted tapers, and pegged dinner candles mingled with pillar candles. The candles on the side table have been placed in distressed white wood candlesticks, unlikely but lovely companions to the contemporary electric table lamps they stand between.

Champion the unconventional by building a candle-scape in your fireplace instead of a fire. A chorus of pillar candles in various heights, thoughtfully arranged, gives this formal living-room fireplace a lease on life all summer long.

The wall above the mantel offers another opportunity to diverge from the norm. This hand-painted metal sconce with its intricate scrollwork and five graceful branches replaces the expected framed art.

Candles draw our attention to detail. Bring friends into a candlelit room like this one and they'll appreciate the small touches—the way the ceramic sarsaparilla bottle-vases and proteas seem to grow into the shape of the cream-colored sconce.

If you like the idea of mixing various sizes of pillar candles and would like to keep a candlescape in the fireplace for a while, bear in mind that diameter, at least as much as height, determines how long a candle will burn. When you purchase your candles, be sure to buy enough smaller candles to replace those that burn down.

In the Bedroom

Just as we did when we were children, we come to our bedrooms to sleep, to read, and to play. Set a candle by the bed, and, even unlit, it encourages letting go. Candles and candlelight in the bedroom are visual cues that tell us this is a peaceful, playful place. Little did we know as children that our lives would become so full of demands that we would one day like nothing better than to go to our room. And when you do, you've got candles to light—how nice!

Lovers seem to have an innate appreciation of candlelight's romantic qualities. The human body looks even more beautiful by candlelight. Smiles are more luminous and skin is flawless. Light a two-inch scented pillar, set it on the nightstand, and watch the steady flame reflected in your dear one's eyes. Or create your own starlit paradise with floating candles wandering across the water in a wide-mouthed bowl. ❧ Candles in a bedroom also tell houseguests how much you've been looking forward to their arrival. Your visitor, tired from traveling, sets down her luggage and immediately notices your thoughtfulness—not only have you placed a bouquet of fresh flowers on the dresser, you've also arranged a group of tea lights in front of the mirror. ❧ It's easy to add just the right touches of color and scent with candles too. Line up six deep-plum pillar candles along a windowsill. Mix and match a collection of forties' pottery with equally brightly colored candles. Make a candlescape with small potted cacti and pale-green pillar candles. It's all in the details. If you have a sitting area in your bedroom—with a chaise or just a comfortable, overstuffed chair—candles can make relaxing there even more pleasurable. Use pillar candles in tall wrought-iron stands. Two or three pillars at reading-lamp height can cast plenty of light for reading and a bit of armchair travel. It's kind of fun to imagine what living by candlelight was like for one's nineteenth-century predecessors. Candles can also make a big difference in a home away from home. Bring a travel candle on the road with you to warm up even the plainest hotel accommodations. ❧ Candlelight's soothing constancy can be particularly comforting when you don't feel well. Curl up in bed with a good book, a pot of herbal tea, and light a candle for company. You can burn a four-inch pillar if you like; you've got the time. After all, you're not going anywhere today. ❧ Candles can also make breakfast in bed even more of a perk. Bring in the breakfast tray loaded with fresh-squeezed juice and favorite bakery goodies—and the cheerful, shimmering lights of votive candles in small glass cylinders nestled in among the coffee mugs. Whether the sun comes in to greet you or your eyes meet only the somber gray of a winter's day, you'll be in the lap of luxury—and light. ❧

A romantic bedroom is made even more so with the addition of candlelight. Here, God truly is in the details. On an ornate dresser, mesh cylinder sleeves veil glass votive cups, echoing the ethereal organza of a canopy bed. A metalwork sconce above the writing table reiterates the paradisiacal pattern on the bedspread. An antique copper cooking vessel safely holds a flotilla of floating candles.

The two sizes of pillar candles on the writing table are both aromatherapy candles, a mix of patchouli and cedarwood. This sensual combination brings together the sweet woodsy scent of cedar and the smoky scent of patchouli, a member of the mint family that is considered an aphrodisiac.

When selecting candle-sticks, don't be afraid of the unique, such as the African candlestick used here with a rustic taper candle.

Though clearly expressing a masculine aesthetic, this master bedroom also invites candles and candlelight. With its array of unusual collections of natural objects and photographs, the room encourages breaking the rules—mixing pillar and taper candles in one setting—which further expresses the joie de vivre that inspired its eclectic and very personal decor.

For a good part of the year, most fireplaces go unused. A metal votive cup screen, like the one shown here, is a great warm-season alternative, offering the splendor of a roaring fire without the heat. Forged floor-standing candle holders contribute more to the rustic style.

Remember not to place pillar candles too close to flammable objects or too close to one another. Pillar candles that are placed too near one another can cause neighboring candles to melt. A good rule of thumb is to allow two inches between each candle.

An arrangement of three pillar candles in varying sizes, including one with three wicks, transforms a bamboo side table. Take note, however, that if you're using a pillar candle with multiple wicks, you'll want to burn it long enough so that the pools of wax at the base of each wick connect. This three-wick candle has a lifetime of about 120 hours. Ideally, it should burn for at least five hours each time it's lit.

Filled jar candles randomly spaced along the triptych of windows further the amorous aesthetic as they lightly scent the air. A trio of pillar candles glows with the same gentle exuberance as the yellow rosebuds displayed in a silver mint julep cup next to a cozy chaise longue with which they've been paired.

This bedroom, on the second floor of a three-story Victorian home, has a feminine spirit, which is accentuated by the candles and candleholders. Rosebuds on a painted metal sconce holding two ivory-colored peg candles carry out the rose pattern of the bedding and the bedside arrangement.

Unexpectedly, taper candles in silver candlesticks have been brought from the dining room table to the bedside tables for an unabashedly romantic statement. Though the bedside lamps are electric, their turn-of-the-century style complements the candlelit setting.

Natural objects, such as the whole walnuts that surround the tea lights in this display, can take on new roles. The tea lights are passengers in a brass canoe-shaped candle-holder that's finished in bronze. Candles can also be expressive; the larger pillar candles on this mantel add to the beauty of the room, whether they're lit or not.

The gentle light of late afternoon doesn't compete at all with the candlelight in this bedroom. By day, the bedroom is often the best room in the house to get a few minutes of quality time alone. Honor yourself with candlelight.

Taper candles, like the dozen here that stand in for a fire in their simple glass cubes, are a practical choice for bedrooms. Taper candles don't require the attention that pillar candles do. They can be burned for briefer periods of time and are often dripless. Some are even self-extinguishing.

Whether the effect is real or imagined, almost everyone seems to respond to certain scents. Lime blossom is one of them, refreshing the mind with its clean, citrusy fragrance. The lime blossom aromatherapy candles in this uncluttered room reside in creamy yellowstone holders.

This open, airy bedroom makes it easy to appreciate the spare sensibility of the Japanese. A stalk of bamboo, an understated Buddhist sculpture, and a few pillar candles in simple holders sit atop a cedarwood tansu, helping to make this room a restful place for body and mind.

Aromatherapy— A Sensual Experience

The Egyptians discovered that certain botanical oils placed on the skin had therapeutic results, and for centuries essential oils were only used topically. Only in the last ten years have candles containing these same botanical oils been introduced. Essential oils dispensed into the air seem to have the same therapeutic value that they do when applied to the skin. We also know that because the olfactory bulb is located so near the brain, scents aren't processed in the same way as stimuli effecting the other four senses. As a result, scents often stimulate memories and trigger other powerful sensations. A few drops of essential oil in a warm bath can indeed be beneficial, and burning an aromatherapy candle at the same time enhances the experience.

For instance, if you've ever spent time in a garden rife with lavender, you know how those fragrant wands of tiny purple flowers can seem to set your mind at ease. Burning a lavender aromatherapy candle might well help you have a more restful night. Chamomile is also known for its calming effects, and ylang-ylang, which has a honeyed, heady fragrance, is exceptionally sensual. If you're looking for a pick-me-up instead of a settle-me-down, you might want to light a lemongrass aromatherapy candle. It's always rejuvenating. Honor yourself. Take the time to light an aromatherapy candle. Then, turn down the lights and relax.

Sitting on the same wide sill of the casement windows are two citron candles. Most dinner candles have a ⅞-inch diameter, which is exactly what most candlesticks, including the metal ones pictured, accommodate. A dinner candle with a larger diameter like this one can be custom-fitted by using a candle shaver. One that's a bit too small can be made to fit snugly by using a candle sticker—a sticky wax circle that fits inside the base of a candlestick.

All the candles in this guest bedroom, including the larger pillar candles on the small table in front of the window seat—a birdcage in a former life—are strongly striated, so each candle is intentionally individual.

Emphasize particular details of a room by decorating with candles in complementary shapes and colors that naturally pull attention to those elements. Here, beeswax and paraffin candles, in a medley of hues and forms, stand side by side in leaf-shaped porcelain holders, turning our attention to the framed photographs, the floral-printed upholstery, the jewel-like bedside clock, and the diamond-shaped lights of the windows.

Elevated on wooden holders, three bedside pomegranate pillar candles and a triple-wick pillar candle emphasize the deep oxblood hue of the leather furniture. The triple-wick candle is nestled in a bed of polished stones that fill the footed bowl. In candlelight, the ordinary appears extraordinary: The glass of water reflects the beautiful palette of colors around it.

A wall-mounted sconce—one of the oldest candle accessories—doubles the gift of a dark blue dinner candle by mirroring its crisp, vertical figure and bright flame.

As modern as this sophisticated urban bedroom is, it still conveys an appealing warmth. This is partly the effect of the rich velvet fabric, but it's the generous use of candles that contributes most to the intentional atmosphere.

Stems of cymbidium orchids have been arranged in an opaque ceramic vase on a night table next to a forties-era tulip-shaped reading lamp—the room's only electric fixture. By placing other objects just so, in this case beneath the sconce and next to a burning pillar candle, they can appear aflame themselves.

Transforming Your Bath

Bathrooms are ready-made for candles. Most have windowsills to frame them and mirrors to reflect their steady flames; many have tile countertops to serve as backdrops for candlescapes. Candles can turn almost any bathroom into a serene retreat, especially if it happens to come equipped with that marvelous indoor pool, the bathtub.

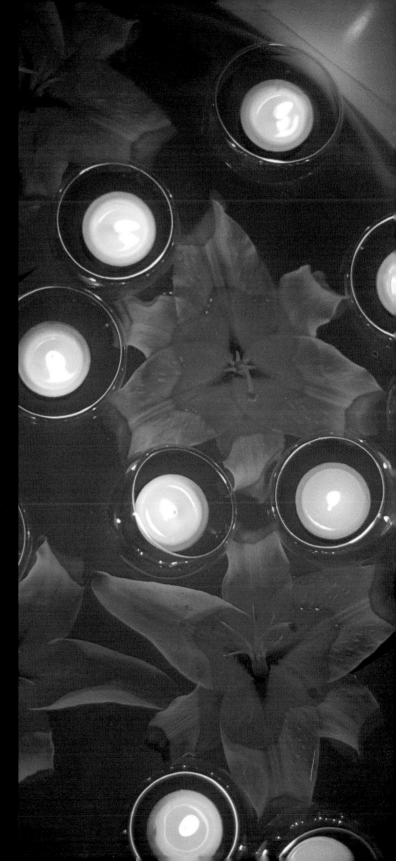

Given the pace and pressures of our daily lives, it's no wonder more and more of us are combining stress relief with personal hygiene, locking the bathroom door, filling the tub, and taking refuge therein. The bath at the end of the day can be a saving grace. Since candlelight seems to have the miraculous ability to slow us down, it only adds to the soothing potential of a long, languorous bath. How natural to pair the calming medium of soft light with the gentle embrace of warm, healing water. ❧ If you're fortunate enough to have a wide ledge around your bathtub, gather up all those votives you were saving for a party and surround your tub with them. Otherwise, set as many as you can on the corners of your tub and on the countertop. Draw your bath, turn off the light, and watch the small flames grow drunk with steam. Candlelight and water are a mystical combination: Here is your own private moonlit lake. Next time, try pillar candles or even dinner candles—why not bring in the candelabra from the dining room table? ❧ Aromatherapy candles, which incorporate essential oils, make bath time even more heavenly and healthful. There are countless fragrances available—everything from lemongrass to sandalwood. Scented candles, which contain perfumes rather than essential oils, are another option. Vanilla, lilac, peach—just name your favorite scent, and you're likely to find it. Many scented candles are saturated with color as well, so you can choose a color and scent to suit your mood. Of course, there's the practical side to aromatherapy and scented candles: They're much better at freshening rooms than room fresheners. ❧ Decorating your bathroom with candles means playing with color, shape, and fragrance. Match them to towels that complement or contrast with your wall color: lavender towels and candles in a lavender bathroom, or red, apple-scented candles in a kiwi-colored room. Arrange artful, geometrically shaped candles in a Japanese-style room. You can find candles shaped like flowers or leaves, and you can mix floating candles with floating blossoms. Vary your candles with the season, or with the celebration. Extend the mood of a Halloween party into the bathroom by filling the tub with water and a fleet of floating pumpkin-shaped candles. ❧ The best thing about candlelight in the bathroom? It's so unexpected. ❧

Bring candlelight into the bathroom in small but lucid ways. Here, cut-metal containers hold colored-glass votive cups. Highlighting the more exotic decor of this bathroom, they also protect the wooden vanity and pay homage to the graceful lilies.

With its geometric tiles and high ceiling, this bath evokes the magnificent tiled baths of Turkey. For centuries, Turks have gone to communal baths not only to bathe but also to enjoy the company of others. Turkish baths, with their intricately tiled interiors and vaulted ceilings, were traditionally lit softly like this—it's so conducive to relaxation.

Bathrooms as artful as this one call out for candles rich in color. The tall aromatherapy pillar candles lining the ledge are infused with essential oils. The shorter pillar candles are unscented.

Complementing the arabesque pattern of the tilework, several cut-out brass votive holders have been placed along the edge of the tub. Though colored glass cups have been used here, clear glass would also work wonderfully.

Color
Therapy

With all the attention aromatherapy has received in the last few years, you would think that smell was an independent sense, acting autonomously from our other four. Not so: Open one door of perception and the others open too. The vibrations we receive through our sense of smell, for instance, often evoke certain colors and vice versa. That's why an apple-scented candle may conjure up a visual memory of the orchard you played in as a child. And that's why, for the most part, we prefer the scents of clear, brightly colored flowers, fruits, and spices and dislike the aromas of things with dark or muddy colors, such as rubber or vinegar. Researchers of the energetic side of human life believe that aroma molecules not only carry chemical messages that spur certain conscious and unconscious reactions, but they also have certain vibrations. These vibrations fit into the electromagnetic spectrum we usually associate with color.

Just as different fragrances of botanical essences appear to affect us in different ways, so do "color essences." Certain aromas are believed to have an affinity for certain colors. Plants are said to have certain color "signatures." For instance, chamomile's signature color is blue. If you were to take a bath in this bathroom, you might want to put a few drops of chamomile in the water. Deep blue is thought to be cooling and relaxing, inspiring understanding and intuitiveness. Chamomile encourages patience and calmness, relaxing the emotions and mind; the combination of the two could be doubly effective. Pairing aromas and colors is at the heart of color therapy. Some candle makers are aware of this, and select the color for an aromatherapy candle based on the fragrance.

An antique chair sports an enamel pitcher and a volume of fragrant lilac branches. Here again, color is the native language, and the glowing ring of melon-colored votive candles in clear glass cups, as well as the tubful of floating candles, affably amplify the yellow, mauve, and periwinkle hues.

A fir floor and a clawfoot tub were all that distinguished this smaller bathroom until candlelight brought it to life. The next time you entertain, don't forget to dress up the bathroom with candles.

In the tub, large and small floating candles in a mixed palette have been set adrift with the colored glass balls traditionally used by fishermen to float their nets. These glass orbs occasionally wash ashore near fishing villages along the coasts of Greece and Mexico. Here, you might find them in gift and flower shops.

If you're fortunate enough to have a backyard hot tub like this, light it and the way to it with candles. Lining the path through the garden are a score or more of small terra-cotta pots. Each pot is filled with pebbles to secure a frosted votive cup.

Candlelight only enhances the pleasures of relaxing outdoors, and on a moonless night or a foggy day, candles can stand in for a heavenly body.

More garden pots have been set all around the wooden decking at a safe distance from the tub itself (so that getting in and out will not be difficult). Here, each pot has once again been filled with small pebbles, giving a solid footing not only to a votive candle in a glass votive cup but also to a large hurricane lamp. Shiny leaves from a nearby lemon tree have been tucked between the edge of the hurricane lamp and the pot.

Retaining elements of the Victorian bath it once was, this bathroom called for a few more formal touches. For instance, the floor-standing ceramic candlesticks might be more expected in a grand ballroom. Most of the cues for the candles and accessories in this bathroom were taken from the marble tub and floor. The mottled white ceramic orchid pots mimic it, as does the shell potpourri on the bath-side table.

Unadorned tea lights are nestled in a potpourri of seashells on a silver-plated tray. Cast in the shimmery light of the tea lights, the shells, with their many scallops, turrets, and costae, can be seen as the tiny architectural shapes they naturally are. The pearlescent interior of the abalone shell underscores the quiet palette of the walls and marble, and makes a perfect receptacle for the melting wax of a tea light.

Sanctuary

Everyone needs to take sanctuary from time to time. For some, being in nature under a sheltering sky is ideal; for others, sanctuary is a quiet and familiar place at home, away from the busyness and stresses of the world. That place might be a corner of a bedroom, an alcove, a breakfast table, a shady spot in the garden, or even an attic. It makes no difference, so long as it's a space that invites contemplation. Candlelight, perhaps more than any other single element, can help to create that.

Unlike artificial lighting, candlelight is not diffused, so by lighting a candle in your sanctuary, you instantly create a focal point for your attention. Attention, of course, is what meditation is all about: attending to the stillness of your inner spirit. A meditation practice might be as basic as following the movement of your breath while letting your eyes rest on the steady flame of a candle. When you close your eyes, the image of the burning candle remains on your retinas; it's as if by staring into the calming flame of a candle, we locate a mirror image of that candle inside ourselves, in the real sanctuary. ❧ A personal altar, no matter how elegant or modest, is a wonderful way to furnish your space. It's a fitting place for not only candles, but also for flowers, photographs, special keepsakes, and talismans. On the other hand, you might prefer things to be more spare: a chair facing a pillar candle and a few fresh flowers set on a windowsill, or a trio of votive candles in an otherwise dark alcove. ❧ Having a timeless connection to the spirit, candles are by their very nature ceremonial; nearly every religious tradition weds candles to spiritual activities. In the Catholic church, worshipers initiate a prayer by kneeling and then lighting a votive candle, to give wings to the prayer. To mark the eight days of Chanukah, Jewish families use a menorah, a candelabra with nine arms. Only one candle, the *shamus*, is allowed to be lit with a match; each night, the *shamus* candle is used to light another one of the other eight candles. In a symbolic New Year's ceremony, Buddhists in Japan and Thailand place lighted candles on leaves or paper boats and set them adrift in a stream. Today, incandescent light has superseded candlelight almost everywhere, except in places where people come, either alone or together, to worship or meditate. ❧ Whether emanating from a single pillar candle or a wall of tea lights, candlelight both stands in for and silently calls out to the spirit, deepening and inspiring everyday rituals such as praying or chanting or writing in a journal. You might even want to elevate ordinary tasks such as ironing or bill paying by lighting a candle. Even something as commonplace as having a daily cup of tea by candlelight can offer solace to the postmodern spirit. In fact, there may be no simpler antidote for stress than lighting a candle and carving a few quiet moments out of the day. ❧

Forgo the fire and tend to your soul instead. This multi-color tile fireplace has been transformed into an altar: a candle altar with a Japanese bowl gong, ceramic vases, calla lilies and parrot tulips, and a wooden tray of votive candles aflame in green-glass votive cups. Pillar candles of differing heights and hues complete the metamorphosis.

Votive candles in amber-tinted glass cups are placed everywhere in this corner of the garden. On the altar, they're carefully positioned with the polished stones. Arranging stones (think of England's Stonehenge), sometimes in small towerlike structures, is a ritual as old as mankind.

Even if all you have time to do is step outside into your garden, communing with nature is always good for the soul. With a little effort, you can create a sanctuary for the spirit, like this one. It's as easy as setting out a dozen or so candles in a shady corner of your garden.

Votive candles have long been used in religious ceremonies throughout the world. Here, they're planted in the garden and on a stone altar, helping to awaken in us a sense of quiet awe: one of those mystic moments that at their most profound are referred to as numinous experiences. The angel has a ready-made candleholder to light the way into meditation.

It may be more difficult to be a Buddhist monk in, say, Silicon Valley than in a remote mountain village, but it's not impossible. The designer of this understated home took his cues from the Japanese and carried a spare Zen aesthetic throughout the house. With candle-light punctuating the clean, conscientious design elements, the whole house feels like a sanctuary.

Here, a stick of sage incense rests in a porcelain holder. Sage is traditionally burned in many cultures, as it's said to clear a space (and a heart) of negative energy. If you can't find a scented candle that suits your taste, incense is always an option. Like candles, incense varies in quality; the best is hand-dipped and scented with essential oils from flowers and herbs.

The mottled surface of the large rustic pillar candles arranged on the altar is created by dipping the warm wax in cold water after it's been hand-poured. More of these uniquely colored pillar candles have been placed on a bookshelf.

Thich Nhat Hahn, the well-known Buddhist monk, has a saying: "Peace is every step." Practicing a walking meditation is made easy here, where metal lanterns with frosted glass panes line the stairway: There's a light urging you to be mindful of each step you take.

A shelf, which is actually the side of a large fireplace, has been turned into a candle altar. Two zafus, the meditation cushions used to sit zazen, wait on a second stairway shelf.

Rather than electric spotlights, you might consider using individual votive candles, as did the collectors of these photographs, to illuminate framed works of art. Without a doubt, candles (in glass votive cups) pay greater homage to both the images and the image maker.

A painted, hand-carved wooden altar brought back from the South Pacific holds a treasury of personally meaningful objects, fruit, a photograph, and flowers in an ever-changing offering of thankfulness and awareness. A combination of pillar candles and votive candles in tinted glass cups stands guard.

A handmade meditation cushion from Kashmir, India, sits at the foot of the altar. A personal sanctuary like this one not only helps to keep memories alive, but also gives us a special place in which to visualize our dreams. Candles illuminate this sanctum with a light that brings heaven to earth.

How to Select and Burn a Pillar Candle

When selecting a pillar candle, you'll first want to consider quality. The best are made with pure food-grade paraffin wax that's hand poured into molds. Denser than machine-made pillars, they burn more cleanly. A hand-poured candle is easy to recognize. When you look at the bottom, you'll see rings resembling the growth rings of a tree. Each ring represents a separate pouring. As a hand-poured candle cools, the chandler "pokes" the wax to release air pockets. You'll also want to consider the size of the pillar candle. You can figure that a high-quality pillar candle will burn one hour for every inch of diameter. In other words, if you purchase a three-inch-wide pillar candle, be prepared for a long-term relationship.

To get the full value from a pillar candle, burn it until the resulting pool of wax extends to the edge of the candle every time you light it. If you do not burn it long enough, the size of the wax pool will become the size of the hole in the candle…forever. When burning pillar candles with multiple wicks, burn them long enough so the pool of wax from each wick connects. When grouping pillar candles in candlescapes, be sure not to place them too close to one another; the heat from one candle can cause its neighbor to drip. Setting pillar candles a couple of inches apart is ideal. As with all candles, burn your pillar candle with respect for its flame: Don't leave a burning candle unat-

tended, burn away from any flammable materials, and in a draft-free area. Keep the wax pool clear of debris such as match heads and wick trimmings, and keep the wick trimmed to ¼ inch. When a pillar candle has burned down to just an inch or so in height, consider it spent.

An eccentric wire sconce houses a single votive candle and points to the unconventional shapes in this personal sanctuary, a room that seems larger than it actually is. The oversized candles and accessories have a surprising effect—in fact, just the opposite of the expected. The vibrant geometric shapes serve as counterpoints to one another, and in their boldness give this tiny nook a spacious feeling.

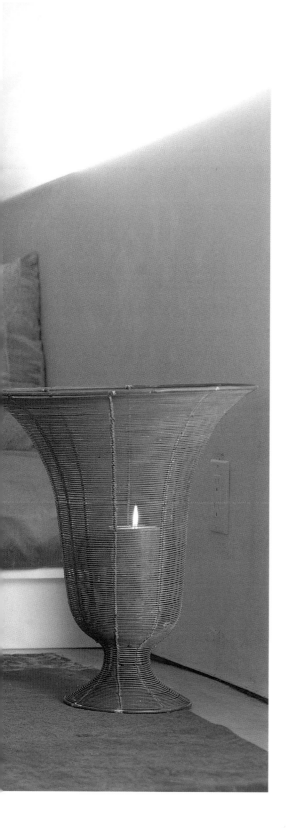

Lighting the Seasons

It is only natural for our eyes to look to light for guidance. At the end as well as at the beginning of life, we are said to move toward light. A light at the end of a dark tunnel, an unusually brilliant star in the sky, a single candle burning in a window—all beckon. For eons, humans have lit their way with fire. Cave dwellers lit the entrances to their homes with torches. Just as lighthouses have always guided ocean-tossed ships safely toward shore, candles and lanterns have shown the way to weary strangers and dear guests alike, all year round.

Every spring, after weeks of harsh weather, as we feel the sun's warm touch, we open our doors and windows. Still, the days are not quite long enough, and we look to extend them and offer a welcome to friends with the gift of candlelight. As daffodils and tulips arise like new thoughts and blossoms cover the fruit trees, highlight their awakening by illuminating small areas of your garden with candlelight. Place a big lantern in an empty birdbath or line a half-dozen small ones along a railing beneath the old apple tree or up a flight of stairs. ❧ Summer is a vast arc of blue space and billowy clouds, jazz pouring through a neighbor's open window, and, come evening, the winsome chirping of crickets. In summer, we live so much more of our lives outdoors. We move meals and parties from the dining room to the patio or garden. And we celebrate graduations, weddings, Father's Day, the Fourth of July—and all the simple pleasures that long days and warm nights grant us. ❧ Balmy evenings spent with friends in the garden sharing good food and wine beg for candlelight. Hang small copper lanterns around a patio umbrella, place a tea light in colored glass at every place setting, or imitate moonlight on the lake with oversized floating candles in the pool. Even if your whole outdoor space is just a small balcony or rooftop, you can add romance to a summer night by setting a tiny table dressed up with a pair of dinner candles. ❧ Much of fall's story is about harvest and its blessings. Wax pumpkins and candle apples that look just like the real thing add an extra dash of spirit to Halloween night. ❧ Symbolically and literally, candlelight creates warmth, which is why it seems so right in winter. There's no reason to take a traditional approach, however. For instance, candles in the snow are a wonderful departure. Place candles in buckets of ice, or line pathways to the house with small lanterns hanging from poles above the snow. Replace electric lights with candles and create your own holiday enchantment. And a candle set in the window on a stormy winter night will send a message of universal love to the lonely wayfarer. ❧

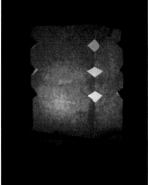

Scissors, a tea light, a paper bag, and a little sand to weigh it down—that's all you need to make the most original of all outdoor lights, the luminaria. Fold a bag and cut into, but not all the way across it. Open it up, roll down the top to make a cuff, add some sand, and put a tea light, or votive cup and candle, in the center. Then, see the light shine through the wonderfully random geometry you've created.

Lantern globes, in two sizes and shapes, have been placed all around the pool, where they are reflected in the water like moons plucked from the sky. Vase lanterns like these consist of a very hard wax outer shell and an inner candle; once the candle burns down, you can continue to bask in the lantern's gentle glow by replacing it with a tea light. Like the pool area, the entire exterior of this two-story home is lit solely by candlelight.

Small glass and copper lanterns have been hung by their handles from metal hooks attached to the frame of the canvas umbrella. Great at protecting their light source from wind, lanterns are ideal for outdoor use; when not being used, however, they should be stored inside.

A good rule of thumb for votive candles: Go for the biggest effect you can imagine with as many votive candles as you think you'll need, and then double the number. You can never use too many, and because even those of the very best quality are priced quite reasonably, you can afford to be extravagant. Outline a walkway, perch them on a deck rail, or surround an outdoor spa like the one pictured here.

Avoid putting new votive candles on top of spent ones. If the metal pieces used at the bottom of votive candles meet, they can become very hot, causing even the most substantial votive container to crack. Fortunately, wax contracts when it gets cold, making it much easier to remove. Put spent votive candles (in their containers) in the freezer; by morning, the old wax will come out easily.

Landings can offer wonderful views and out-of-the-way sitting areas—and are a good place, especially for older family and friends, to catch a breath on the way up the stairs. This teak bench beckons with wooden sconces and wooden lanterns, while the landing and the stairs themselves have been illuminated with votive candles elevated a few inches on metal pedestals.

Welcome guests—and the ghosts and goblins of your choice—by hallowing your house with candlelight. Here, floating candles that look exactly like small pumpkins bob in a copper tub.

Rather than lining the walkway, several copper lanterns are suspended from garden stakes collected together. Inside, the house is filled with masses of pillar scapes of various heights and groupings of dinner candles.

Guests will have to look very closely in order to tell what's faux and what's real among the myriad pumpkins greeting them at this house. Both carved jack-o'-lanterns and grinning wax pumpkins, aglow with light from votive candles in votive cups, lead the way up the steps and onto the front porch.

Fire and ice—if ever two opposites were meant for each other, it's these two. The snow that's been cleared from the pathway to this mountain retreat has been scooped into buckets—the ordinary galvanized type you can find at any hardware store—painted red and planted with bright red tapers. The candles, stuck into the snow, are protected from the weather by tall glass hurricane lamps.

More painted buckets sit atop the porch railing. These brim with snowball sculptures; more candles, tea lights, burn behind and within the sculptures, turning them into magical, miniature fire-and-ice palaces.

After weeks of cold, what a joy it is to fling open the doors to spring! Whether you're expecting houseguests, a friend for lunch, or no one at all, honor the light that makes this reawakening possible with your own luminous offering.

What a pleasure to walk down this garden path. Small and large lily-white pillar candles are set on simple copper-colored metal plates all along the way, each dreamlike behind a copper mesh sleeve.

Votive candles, opalescent in milk-glass votive cups, are set along one of the main beams of this bungalow-style porch. The porch reaches out into the garden and becomes a trellis for a wisteria vine, blooming with lush, spiraling purple blooms—and for more candles to herald earth's annual rebirth.

Candle Tips and Candle Care

Burning a candle is not a science but an art. Following a few "rules" will help you get the most value out of every candle you burn. Remember: A candle is fire, so be safe; be there to watch it burn. Keep an eye on the flame. Make sure it's still; a flickering flame may look pretty, but it means that you should move your candle. Drafts can cause candles to smoke and burn unevenly. Be sure to keep candles out of the reach of children, and burn them on nonflammable surfaces. Keep debris, such as matches and wick trimmings, out of the wax pool. Make sure the wick is centered in the candle, and before lighting or relighting the candle, trim it to ¼ inch. There are self-trimming wicks that curl at the top as the candle burns; the curled-over portion evaporates, ensuring that the wick is never longer than ¼ to ⅜ inch.

Candles depend on oxygen; even a high-quality candle will smoke if it isn't getting enough. A small, closed room is not the place to burn a candle. The best way to extinguish a candle is with a snuffer, but if you don't have a snuffer, there's another option. Put two fingers out sideways in front of the candle and close enough so that you can't see the flame (about an inch away), then blow, not at the candle, but at your fingers. The air will jump over your fingers and onto the flame. If you've purchased paraffin candles that you don't plan on burning right away, be sure to store them in a cool dry, place. Don't refrigerate them, as this will cause quality paraffin candles to crack (they're made from pure, clean wax and not "glued" together with fillers or animal fats). Putting spent votives in the freezer overnight, however, is a great trick. The cold wax contracts, pulling away from the holders, so it's easy to remove.

Ingredients

PARAFFIN

Until the beginning of the nineteenth century, candles were made of fats and beeswax. The discovery of paraffin revolutionized candle-making. A by-product of petroleum refining, paraffin is further refined when it is used with food products, such as in the coatings for milk cartons and Gouda cheese. The best candles are made with this same highly refined paraffin, because as it's refined, it becomes denser and longer burning, constituting an excellent fuel source. And for people with allergies, candles made with paraffin are a better choice than beeswax candles.

FRAGRANCE

Most fragrances are not compatible with wax or flame, so fragrance oils must be carefully selected and tested to ensure good results. Fragrances are not only distinguished by quality but also by density. For instance, three percent of a powerful fragrance is preferable to ten percent of a less potent fragrance, as the greater the percentage of fragrance in a candle, the more likely it is to smoke. The best filled candles use more concentrated fragrances in smaller quantities.

WICKS

It's the wax, of course, that fuels a candle, and the wick literally wicks up this fuel and delivers it to the flame. For the most part, a good-quality candle will have either a paper or cotton wick; it will also have a wick that's neither too thin nor too thick. When a wick is too thin, the pool of wax will not reach the edge of the candle, reducing the burn time and value of the candle. When the wick is too thick, it feeds the flame too quickly, causing the melted wax to drip over the sides of the candle. To produce a balanced candle, a chandler must often test a dozen or more wicks.

CANDLE FLAME

Though a dancing flame is both romantic and mesmerizing, you'll find that a still one can be even more mysterious—and so much safer and cleaner. A still flame also lengthens your candle's life and ensures that it will burn without dripping or smoking. So, if the candle flame is moving, relocate the candle or eliminate the draft.

PILLAR CANDLES

These cylindrical candles come in many different diameters, heights, colors, and even scents. The best pillar candles are hand-poured. Hand-poured candles are more dense than machine-made ones, so they burn more cleanly. When you look at the bottom of a hand-poured pillar you'll see rings that look much like the rings of a tree. Each ring represents a separate pouring. As a hand-poured candle cools, the candle maker "pokes" the wax to release air pockets. This makes for a denser, higher-quality candle that burns longer and without smoke.

types of candles
Glossary

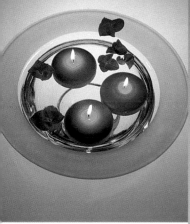

FLOATING CANDLES

Unlike pillar candles, the best floating candles are pressed rather than poured. Pressed floating candles are dense and long-burning—and easy to spot. The top of a well-made pressed floating candle is not flat but convex. Conversely, a poured floating candle is flat on top and looks as if it was made in a muffin tin. Floating candles are intended for use in water-tight, nonflammable vessels. As safe as they are captivating, floating candles are a wise choice for the bedroom. Because they are often incorporated into centerpieces at the table, floating candles are usually unscented, so that no fragrance competes with the aroma and flavor of the food.

TAPER CANDLES

Distinguished by their streamlined design, a taper candle generally narrows at the top from a ⅞-inch-diameter bottom. Because they come in a standard size, finding a candleholder to fit one is easy. Neither poured nor pressed, a taper candle is the result of a wick's being dipped in warm wax numerous times. It can take as many as thirty dips to produce one taper candle. Tapers are generally used on the table, and because food and fragrance don't mix, they are almost always unscented. One-half-inch and ¼-inch sizes are also available and are used primarily in floral arrangements.

DINNER CANDLES

Distinguished by their straight-sided design, dinner candles are almost always extruded. The warm wax, which looks like icing squeezed from a decorating tube, is cut into lengths averaging about twelve inches. Dinner candles are easier to produce than dipped or poured candles and so offer a very economical option. You can have dinner by candlelight for as little as ten cents a day—as long as you're burning your candles properly. A dinner candle can be used with a candle follower: a ring that holds a shade (to diffuse the candlelight) and slides down the candle as it burns.

FILLED CANDLES

The amount of fragrance a candle delivers is in direct proportion to the pool of wax exposed to the air. Because filled candles are made by being poured into their containers, manufacturers can use low-melting-point waxes that liquefy more quickly, thereby exposing a larger pool of wax. Thus, filled candles are the most efficient way to fill a room with fragrance. Also, because the wax has a container holding it together, a filled candle can contain greater amounts of fragrance than can a pillar candle. The greater the percentage of fragrance oils in a candle, the greater the tendency of the wax to liquefy. Filled candles are also available without scent.

VOTIVE CANDLES

Votive candles are designed to liquefy, so they must be burned in containers that can hold the liquefied wax. Because they're small, votive candles are easily scented and are second only to filled candles as a way to add fragrance to the home. Used in multiples, scented or unscented, they're also a wonderful way to bring lots of candlelight into any room instantly and economically. Burned indoors or out, a high-quality votive will burn for ten hours or more.

TEA LIGHTS

Like votive candles, tea lights liquefy when they're burned. They come in metal holders, usually made of aluminum, that contain the liquid wax as it burns. Because they don't require a separate holder, tea lights are more versatile than votive candles and can be used in many environments. Both scented and unscented tea lights are available. Because it's designed to liquefy, the wax that's used in tea lights can be much less refined, so it's important to buy them from a reputable source and to replace any that smoke. A well-made tea light 1 inch in diameter will burn for about five hours.

CHANDELIERS

The first chandeliers were actually thirteenth-century coronas: iron hoops with prickets that held no more than three or four candles. King George III of England receives credit for the more elaborate chandelier. The king had a penchant for candles, and the chandeliers that hung above his royal feasts held whole constellations of them. Not every chandelier is elaborate. Depending on its style, a chandelier can add the flavor of a western ranch house, a medieval castle, or a Buddhist temple to a room. But whether it's lighting an entry hall or a dining table, a chandelier both brightens and enlivens the space.

SCONCES

These traditional wall-mounted lighting fixtures enhance almost any decor. A basic sconce consists of a mounting bracket, an arm, a platform, or a shield of glass or metal. The implementations of these elements are as varied as the imagination, but the best are designed to safely cradle candles or oil lamps while adding dramatic light-and-shadow accents to a room. Every sconce makes a statement. Classic designs typically appear very utilitarian. More modern designs are frequently bold expressions of style.

holders and
accessories

TAPER STAKES

Not so easy to find, but well worth the search, taper stakes make it possible to burn taper candles in the garden—and not just on a table. These tall elegant outdoor accessories have a pointed end that is easily secured in the soil. Place several stakes along a path or in a circle around a plant you'd like to highlight. With their heat-resistant glass cylinders, taper stakes have minimal metal, so all your eye focuses on is the bright burning taper candle inside. In order to protect the flame from the wind, the cylinder needs to be taller than the taper placed inside it.

LANTERNS

A beautiful way to prevent unwelcome breezes or drafts from extinguishing pillar candles both outdoors and in, lanterns come in many sizes, shapes, and materials, including glass, metal, and wood. There are primarily two kinds of lanterns: those with a hinged door that swings open to allow the candle to be lit or changed, and those that have a one-piece chimney that either lifts up or off. The latter is a hurricane lantern, the predecessors of which were once used on sailing ships. Many of today's box-shaped lanterns are modeled on Japanese lanterns; many round hanging lanterns are derivations of Chinese designs. Lanterns are used with votive candles as well as tea lights.

HURRICANES

A hurricane lamp has both a practical and a romantic side. It keeps a candle's flame from being extinguished and from burning unevenly in unexpected drafts, and it does so in a most gracious way. At this table, a large fluted glass hurricane lamp acts as an elegant anchor.

CYLINDERS

Not surprisingly, though square candle "cylinders" are available, most are cylindrical in shape, and they are virtually always made of glass. The finest are handblown. They are intended to hold water, so they can lead double lives as vases, but cylinders are particularly enchanting as candleholders when you place river rocks, bits of sea glass, marbles, shells, and/or colored sand in the water, then set a single floating candle or floating oil lamp on the surface.

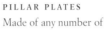

CANDLESTICKS

A candlestick holds a taper, dinner, or peg candle. It raises the steady light of a candle to just above eye level, making these "windows of the soul" more accessible. Almost any material that can be carved or molded has been used to craft candlesticks. Some of the most elegant have been wrought from silver and gold. The earliest candlestick was a small, handheld torch made of slips of bark or wood dipped in tallow and tied together. It was a long time before someone thought to attach a cup at the base to catch the dripping wax, and not until the Middle Ages did the candlestick become more decorative than that.

PILLAR PLATES

Made of any number of nonflammable materials, including glass, stone, bronze, brass, and zinc, a pillar plate is generally a flat disc designed to sit under a pillar candle and to protect the surfaces beneath it. It may sit flat on the surface or be supported by small feet or pedestals. Pillar plates come in a range of circumferences to fit various sizes of pillar candles. There are also square, rectangular, and oblong pillar plates made to fit pillar candles with those shapes or a grouping of several smaller pillar candles.

VOTIVE CUPS

Unlike pillar candles, votive candles liquefy as they burn, so it's necessary to use a cup, rather than a plate. Designed to hold the liquid wax produced by a single votive candle, a votive cup is generally made of glass. Votive is defined as something given or dedicated in fulfillment of a vow or pledge, and votive candles and cups are familiar to many in the context of the Catholic church. The worshiper prays and lights a votive candle, making a votive offering. Votive cups are available in a rainbow of colored glass as well as clear, frosted, and milk glass.

CANDLE SNUFFERS

Essentially, there are two varieties of candle snuffers: a bell-shaped snuffer that basically suffocates the candle flame, and a more archaic scissors-shaped snuffer that pinches the wick, thereby extinguishing the flame. The bell-shaped snuffer is much more widely used. The bell is generally hinged at the end of a long handle, making it easy to reach candles at any angle. A classic pair of nineteenth-century silver candlesticks almost always had a matching snuffer and tray.